LUNCH COUNTER SIT-INS

HOW PHOTOGRAPHS HELPED FOSTER PEACEFUL CIVIL RIGHTS PROTESTS

by Danielle Smith-Llera

Content Adviser: Patrick Jones, Associate Professor, Department of History,
Institute for Ethnic Studies, University of Nebraska-Lincoln

COMPASS POINT BOOKS
a capstone imprint

Compass Point Books are published by Capstone Press,
1710 Roe Crest Drive, North Mankato, Minnesota 56003
www.mycapstone.com

Editorial Credits
Michelle Bisson, editor; Tracy McCabe, designer; Svetlana Zhurkin, media researcher;
Kathy McColley, production specialist; Kathleen Baxter, library consultant

Content Adviser: Patrick Jones, Associate Professor, Department of History, Institute
of Ethnic Studies, University of Nebraska-Lincoln

Photo Credits
Alamy: Philip Scalia, 5, 56, Walter Oleksy, 22, 54 (bottom left); AP Images: Atlanta
Journal-Constitution, 7, Atlanta Journal-Constitution/Charles Jackson, 47, Chicago
Sun-Times, 32, Chuck Burton, 53, Evan Vucci, 29, Harry Harris, 36, Spencer Jones,
34, The Jacksonville Daily News/John Althouse, 15; Bruce Roberts Photography,
cover; Getty Images: Bettmann, 39, Michael Ochs Archives, 50, The LIFE Images
Collection/Donald Uhrbrock, 37, The LIFE Images Collection/Lynn Pelham, 44, The
Washington Post, 20; Granger, 11; Library of Congress: Prints and Photographs
Division, 18, 24, 25, 26, 51, 54 (top and bottom right), 55, 57, Prints and
Photographs Division/Photographs in Carol M. Highsmith's America Project in the
Carol M. Highsmith Archive, 8; Newscom: akg-images, 27, Everett Collection, 42, 48;
Science Source: Bruce Roberts, 14

Library of Congress Cataloging-in-Publication Data
Cataloging-in-publication information is on file with the Library of Congress.
ISBN 978-0-7565-5878-9 (library binding)
ISBN 978-0-7565-5880-2 (paperback)
ISBN 978-0-7565-5882-6 (ebook PDF)

Printed in the United States of America
PA017

TABLEOFCONTENTS

ChapterOne
A SIMPLE REQUEST

Four young men arrived at the Blair home on Sunday night, January 31, 1960. The visit did not seem unusual—at least to those who did not yet know their plan. Ezell Blair Jr. had grown up in Greensboro, North Carolina. He and his three friends went to an all-black college there. The 18-year-old men shared meals, studied together, and stayed up late talking in the dorms of North Carolina Agricultural and Technical State University, nicknamed A&T. But tonight Blair had brought his friends home on urgent business that would change the course of their lives—and make history. He later recalled telling his parents, "We're going to do something tomorrow that's going to shake up the nation." Blair never forgot his father's shock and intense questioning: "Do you guys realize that what you are doing is going to affect not only your families, your friends, [but also] your community? Are you ready for that?"

Blair's friend Joseph McNeil had been ready for weeks. After winter break with family in New York, he had traveled by bus back to college and the trip left him furious. In the northern United States, he enjoyed the same freedoms as other citizens. But at the bus station in Richmond, Virginia, he ordered a

When four young men planned a lunch counter sit-in, the last thing on their minds was the thought that, one day, there would be a monument to them.

David Richmond   Franklin McCain   Ezell Blair, Jr.   Joseph McNeil
(Jibreel Khazan)

FEBRUARY ONE

These four A & T freshmen envisioned and carried out the lunch counter sit-in of February 1, 1960, in downtown Greensboro. Their courageous act against social injustice inspired similar protests across the nation and is remembered as a defining moment in the struggle for civil rights.

hot dog and was refused service because of his skin color. Later that year, the Supreme Court would rule that segregation in stations serving buses traveling between states was unconstitutional. But that was months away, and black citizens knew that new laws were often not enforced. Those laws did not change the attitudes or the injustice they faced. Fear of violence made demanding rights a challenge, even when those rights were protected by the U.S. Constitution. At least 4,000 black people had been murdered in hate crimes since the late 1800s after the abolition of slavery.

McNeil's friends shared his frustrations. For two weeks they debated relentlessly what to do. On January 31 they came up with a plan. "Are you chicken?" McNeil asked Franklin McCain. Raised in Washington D.C., McCain had witnessed slow progress toward desegregation in the nation's capital. "No, man," McCain responded, and poked Blair and David Richmond in the chest, asking the same question. Richmond said he was in. Blair was reluctant at first. But when McCain held a vote, four hands went up. The foursome were now united in their mission.

The four young men met in front of the A&T campus library the next afternoon, February 1, 1960. They dressed for their mission in their best clothes. McCain wore his Air Force ROTC uniform. They walked downtown through a city divided by race. Their own school had been founded in 1891 to keep black students from entering all-white North Carolina State University. The lives of Greensboro's black and white residents rarely overlapped. Black citizens

At least 4,000 black people had been murdered in hate crimes since the late 1800s . . .

The students who sat at the segregated lunch counters were brave. They were also nervous about what might happen.

squeezed into cramped houses in the southeastern neighborhoods of the city where they attended their own churches and schools. White people filled neighborhoods of more expensive houses on the city's northwest side. Both communities frequented stores in Greensboro's busy downtown, but many displayed signs reading "We serve white customers only." Blacks and whites could not sit together in restaurants or movie theaters, or share bathrooms or water fountains.

The men arrived at their destination: a popular two-story store called Woolworth's. Its large, inviting

windows displayed merchandise. The four men knew black customers were welcome to shop. They also knew that black customers were not allowed at the 66-seat lunch counter. Lunch counter service was reserved for white customers.

As planned, the young men bought a few items in the store and then headed for the lunch counter. They sat down on the vinyl-covered stools and ordered pie and coffee. The waitress refused to serve them. They showed their purchase receipts to prove they deserved to be served like other customers. White customers around them grew quiet. The men had set a drama in motion and no one knew what would happen next. The men stayed on their stools, their legs quaking.

A black employee appeared from the kitchen. She knew that segregation ruled the store. She could prepare food for the lunch counter but was not even allowed to wait on customers. She scolded them for making trouble: "Why don't you boys go back to the campus where you belong?"

Lunch counter manager Clarence Harris instructed the waitresses to ignore the men and headed for the police station. Police Chief Paul Calhoun told him that he could only arrest the men if Harris accused them of trespassing. But Harris decided that he would only do that if the protest turned violent. Calhoun did send police officers to monitor the unpredictable situation. They paced behind the lunch counter's stools, tapping their police clubs in their palms.

Returning to Woolworth's frustrated and without a solution, Harris encountered another problem— this one just outside the store. *Greensboro Record* photographer Jack Moebes hoped to get inside with his camera. Harris covered the camera's lens with his hands and ordered Moebes to stay out. Harris closed the lunch counter early and turned off the lights. The four young men marveled that they had not been arrested. They vowed to return. Around 6 p.m.

Moebes photographed the four friends walking back to campus side-by-side.

The four friends returned with 16 other students the next morning. Newspaper reporters, photographers, and television crews were already waiting. The protesters took stools and sat quietly through the busy lunch hour. Some read their textbooks as servers took orders from white customers sitting nearby. "It is time for someone to wake up and change the situation," Blair told reporters, "and we decided to start here." This time Moebes got his photograph of the four protesters seated at the lunch counter. The newspaper, the *Greensboro Record*, announced that the protesters were "seeking luncheon counter service, and will increase their numbers daily until they get it."

That night the student protesters prepared a letter to Woolworth's president. They asked him to take "a firm stand to eliminate this discrimination." By 1960 the Woolworth chain had about 1,000 stores in the U.S., Europe, Africa, and the Caribbean.

Woolworth's headquarters let its stores follow local customs even if that policy allowed stores in the southern U.S. to discriminate against black customers. Support for segregation there was strong. By the third day of the sit-in, white people supporting segregation rushed to Woolworth's early to try to occupy the stools before the protesters could do so.

This photo by Jack Moebes captured the four young men at the lunch counter.

More protesters packed the lunchroom daily, growing to 300 in less than a week. Supporters of segregation taunted them with racial slurs and threatened them with violence. Yet the protesting students, including a few white supporters, sat quietly without responding, despite the anger that they felt. "It wasn't as though we were immune to things that caused people to resort to violence," McCain said, "I fully expected violence." About 1,000 people now packed the store in an uneasy mixture of students, journalists, police officers, and undercover detectives. Others watched outside through store windows. A bomb threat sent frightened people rushing from the store on the sixth day.

Woolworth's closed the lunch counter, which just a week earlier had served 2,000 meals a day. Other Greensboro businesses were losing money too. Student leaders had organized increasing numbers of protesters and taken over other downtown lunch counters. The mayor and business owners had no choice but to meet with black student leaders. Months of difficult negotiations lay ahead.

News and images of the "Greensboro Four" had spread well beyond the city, and, as the news spread, more black students across the South put on their best clothes to take stools at local segregated counters. Ninety miles (145 kilometers) south of Greensboro, Bruce Roberts of Charlotte, North Carolina, would capture the shot of a first-day sit-in because of a tip from a northern source.

When the telephone rang on February 9, 1960, Roberts was the only photojournalist in the office of the North Carolina newspaper, the *Charlotte Observer*. Ray Mackland, an editor with *Life* magazine in New York City, was calling with an exciting tip. Mackland told him a sit-in was about to start at the local Woolworth's lunch counter. Roberts' newspaper gave its prize-winning photographers freedom to do independent projects. Roberts stuffed six rolls of film into his pockets, grabbed his Nikon 35mm camera and lenses, and dashed out the door. He ran most of the two blocks to the Woolworth's

"... white
people
had the
power, the
power of
life and
death ..."

store in Charlotte so as not to miss the sit-in.

The night before, 21-year-old Charles Jones attended a meeting of students at Charlotte's all-black Johnson C. Smith University. The news from Greensboro had inspired Jones, who grew up in a small South Carolina town "where the rules of life were very clear . . . white people had the power, the power of life and death, the power to do whatever they chose to at any given time whenever they wanted to with no consequences at all." He announced a plan: They would order lunch at Woolworth's segregated lunch counter. When more than 200 students volunteered, Jones organized an ambitious protest in eight downtown Charlotte locations at once.

Roberts was astonished to see no crowds gathered. A fire truck was parked nearby, but the firefighters were lounging casually. He rushed into the lunchroom, aiming his wide-angle lens at the long room of seated protesters. Worried that a manager would throw him out, Roberts quickly shot a roll of film, popped it out of the camera, and stashed it safely in his pocket.

Looking around, he realized the entire staff seemed to have left. That meant managers, waitstaff, and cooks. Only the protesters remained, "waiting peacefully to see what would happen." The next day, groups of about 40 students each began protests in segregated stores across the city of Charlotte.

Moebes and Roberts found vastly different
protests at Woolworth's counters. Inside the
Greensboro store, Moebes remembered a mood
so tense it could easily explode into a violent
situation. Roberts, on the other hand, called the
Charlotte protest "one of the quietest things I've ever
photographed." Yet both protests were part of a much
larger story. Within three months, sit-ins started in
more than 55 cities in at least 13 states.

For many photographers—particularly those
living in the South—the struggle for civil rights
was personal. Roberts sent five film rolls to *Life*

FRAMING A NEW WORLD

Bruce Roberts was able to photograph the sit-ins on the spot because of his 35 mm camera.

When Jack Moebes took the first photograph of the Greensboro Four, it was not a quick snapshot. A battery the size of a lunch box was strapped to his hip. It powered his heavy Speed Graphic camera but made him slow-moving. Yet the sturdy camera had been a popular choice for photojournalists since it was introduced in 1912. In the half-century since, photographers carried the hardy camera from studios outside into streets and even into war zones to create prize-winning photographs.

When Bruce Roberts took the first photograph of the Charlotte lunch counter protesters, he was holding a different kind of camera. Since the late 1940s Nikon had been producing a 35mm camera that was lightweight enough to fit into one hand. Roberts had begun his career with a Speed Graphic camera and

remembered having to load a new photographic plate into the camera for each new photograph. But with a roll of film coiled inside a Nikon, he could shoot a long series of photos without taking the camera from his eye. The 35mm "opened up a whole new beautiful world," he remembered. A critical part of this world was light. Moebes' Speed Graphic flashed brilliant light from powerful bulbs. But Roberts, like many other photographers who helped fill the pages of *Life* magazine, preferred soft, natural light. It suited the unstaged, natural moments he preferred. Photographers would turn increasingly to the portable and adaptable 35mm to document civil rights history on location. "Eventually many other photographers could stand at the edges of the scenes and capture what would become a chronicle of the larger story," Roberts said.

magazine on February 9, but he kept one for himself because the protests mattered so much to him. The photographers' published photos helped broadcast the protesters' message. That message was, "You will treat me as a human being with dignity and I will sit here until you decide you have to treat me in that way. America was being taught how human beings are meant to deal with each other," said historian and civil rights activist Vincent Harding.

ChapterTwo
A NEW KIND OF WEAPON

When the Greensboro Four sat down, shocked white customers ignored them—all except one elderly white woman. "Boys, I am so proud of you. I only regret that you didn't do this 10 years ago," McCain recalls her saying. They might have been the first to sit at a Woolworth's counter, but they were not the first black people in America to challenge segregation and racism. In 1892, 30-year-old Homer Plessy sat down in a whites-only train car in New Orleans. When he refused to move, he was arrested.

Plessy was protesting a condition with a long history. For more than two centuries, enslaved Africans and their descendants endured brutal abuse on white-owned plantations in southern states. When the Civil War (1861-1865) broke out, about 180,000 enslaved people joined the Union Army. They hoped that northern states would defeat southern states and end the practice of slavery. Even free black people longed for basic rights such as access to education.

But many southern state governments held on to racist beliefs even after slavery was abolished. In the late 1800s they passed laws that enforced racial segregation. These laws were called Jim Crow laws. Black citizens were discriminated against in many ways. They were forced to sit in the back of trains,

WHEN YOU DRINK A

Dr Pepper

GOOD FOR LIFE!

YOU DRINK A BITE TO EAT

COLORED·ADM.
10c

CASH·NITE
FRIDAY $400

buses, and in cramped movie theater balconies, among many ,other indignities.

In court, Plessy argued that segregation of train cars was unconstitutional. The all-white Supreme Court justices heard his case, *Plessy v. Ferguson.* The Court ruled that it was legal for black and white citizens to live separate lives as long as the facilities were of equal quality. It was well known in the South, but unstated, that these facilities were never equal. Justice Henry Brown stated that segregation was necessary for the "preservation of the public peace

> "Our constitution is color-blind, and neither knows nor tolerates classes among citizens . . . all citizens are equal before the law."

and good order." But John Marshall Harlan, the only justice to disagree with the decision, argued, "Our constitution is color-blind, and neither knows nor tolerates classes among citizens. In respect of civil rights, all citizens are equal before the law." Harlan warned that segregation caused anger and distrust between black and white citizens. He was right.

Segregation caused activists to organize for change. One of the earliest civil rights organizations, the National Association for the Advancement of Colored People (NAACP), was founded in 1909. Its members believed the courtroom was the best place to fight for equal treatment. But some activists wanted changes to come more quickly. In Alexandria, Virginia, in March 1939, a 25-year-old black lawyer named Samuel Tucker requested a library card. Only white people were allowed to use public libraries there, so he was refused. He took the battle for black people to use the library to court. But rather than desegregate the library, white city officials planned construction of a new library for black patrons.

Tucker believed that the new library would be poorly equipped and would offer only old books rejected by the whites-only library. After all, public schools for black students were small, shabby, and inferior to schools for white students. Tucker created a plan to protest this discrimination and recruited volunteers. They would follow the example

The five men who led the sit-in at the Alexandria Library were led out by police.

of protesters who, for a half-century, had stood up to racism with bold defiance while on their best behavior. They hoped that this self-control in the face of arrests sent a powerful message to observers.

Tucker sent five well-dressed young men into the whites-only library to request library cards on August 21, 1939. They were denied, but instead of leaving, they took books from the shelves and sat down to read. A crowd of 300 spectators gathered outside. A journalist's photograph captured all five walking out with a police officer. The city rushed to complete the new library. It was tiny and full of old books, just as Tucker had said.

Black people who moved north still found discrimination: Stores might welcome black customers but refuse to hire black employees. Beginning in the 1920s, black protesters formed picket lines outside these stores to interrupt business. These picket lines urged people to boycott with signs that read, "Don't Buy Where You Can't Work." Boycotts eventually pressured stores to open hundreds of jobs to black citizens in northern cities like Chicago and Cleveland.

But even though business owners and managers were more willing to hire black job applicants, they still were not always willing to allow black customers to eat and mingle with white customers in their restaurants. Even in northern cities that did not permit segregation, black people did not always feel welcome.

James Farmer and fellow activists challenged this injustice with a new kind of protest. In May 1942 the 22-year-old Farmer led a group of 28 University of Chicago students—both black and white—to a restaurant. Staff there had refused to serve him before and had thrown his money on the sidewalk. This time, only white members of Farmer's group were served.

James Farmer (center) was an early civil-rights activist.

They refused to eat and the whole group refused to leave, filling all the restaurant's seats. They had no idea their protest would inspire others, including the Greensboro Four. More than 40 years later, Farmer recalled his thoughts at the time: "If we were lucky, there might be a small paragraph on a back page of the *Chicago Tribune* saying, in effect, that a few nuts and crackpots sat in a restaurant until they were served, or thrown out, or the place closed— whichever came first." Police refused to make arrests since the protesters were not breaking any laws. The restaurant gave in and served Farmer and his group.

Success energized Farmer and his fellow activists. That same year, they formed the Congress of Racial Equality (CORE) and vowed to fight segregation "without fear, without compromise, and without hate." CORE would help spread the idea of nonviolent protests well beyond Chicago.

In the South, a freshman at all-black Howard University had been holding her own sit-ins since 1941. For more than a year, Ruth Powell sat for hours at a time in Washington, D.C., restaurants where staff refused to serve her. In January 1943 Powell and two classmates were overcharged when they ordered hot chocolates at a local shop. They refused to pay the extra amount and were arrested. In April, another Howard law student, Pauli Murray, led three students into a whites-only restaurant. They prepared to be refused service and to stay anyway. More protesters entered and soon filled all the seats. Within 45 minutes, the managers closed the restaurant, so protesters formed a picket line outside. In two days, the restaurant began serving black customers. But many restaurants in the capitol remained segregated.

Other activists preferred fighting segregation in the courtroom. Since 1935 NAACP lawyers had been arguing that segregation did not offer black people choices that were equal to those white people had when it came to schooling, transportation, or housing, for example. But some NAACP members

also recognized the power of confronting racism with peaceful protests. One longtime NAACP leader, Mary Church Terrell, sued a restaurant in Washington, D.C., after being refused service in 1950—the year she turned 87. The Supreme Court ruled in 1953 that all the capital's restaurants had to be integrated.

Terrell lived to see the NAACP win a stunning courtroom victory over segregation the following year. The anti-segregation arguments in Plessy's

Linda Brown and her mother read about the Brown ruling the day the case was won.

case helped NAACP lawyer Thurgood Marshall convince the Supreme Court that segregation was unconstitutional. In *Brown v. Board of Education*, Marshall argued that segregated schools did not offer a separate but equal experience to black children. All nine justices agreed and ruled that segregation was unconstitutional in public schools.

But this new ruling was not implemented for years and inequality remained. Young protesters

Martin Luther King Jr. became perhaps the most powerful voice of the civil-rights movement.

were frustrated with the slow pace of change. It took Terrell's case three years to travel through the court system. On January 20, 1955, Morgan State College students, with the assistance of CORE, held a sit-in at a segregated lunch counter at Read's Drug Store in Baltimore, Maryland. Their results came faster than any courtroom could provide: The entire Read's chain of 39 stores desegregated the next day.

Martin Luther King Jr. and other church leaders from 10 states formed the Southern Christian Leadership Conference (SCLC) in 1957. Their aim

BREAKING LAWS

Mahatma Gandhi's peaceful protests led to India's independence from Great Britain in 1947.

Shortly after Homer Plessy refused to give up his train seat, a young Indian lawyer in South Africa, Mahatma Gandhi, also refused to give up his train seat because of the color of his skin. Gandhi was forced off the train. Discrimination against black South Africans and Indians by white European settlers outraged him, especially since the British ruthlessly ruled his native India. He began to form a plan for resistance. He turned to ancient Indian religions that urged people to avoid harming others. American ideas inspired him too. An essay published in 1849 by American philosopher Henry David Thoreau inspired Gandhi to fight injustice without violence. Thoreau wrote "Civil Disobedience" after a brief stay in a Massachusetts jail for refusing to pay a government tax for a number of reasons, one of which was to protest slavery. Thoreau argued that a person's sense of right and wrong is stronger than a government's laws. Gandhi led boycotts and marches against British rule, demonstrating the power of breaking unjust laws with nonviolence.

Gandhi's ideas echoed through King's words and those of many civil rights leaders. King recalled that "While the Montgomery boycott was going on, India's Gandhi was the guiding light of our technique of nonviolent social change. We spoke of him often." Like Gandhi, King and others accepted jail time as a way to protest without violence and to apply pressure to governments to change unjust laws. A campaign called "Jail-No-Bail" that developed during the lunch counter protests encouraged protesters to choose prison over paying a fine, or bail, to go free. College students peacefully waiting in crowded jail cells attracted news media coverage and national sympathy.

was to spread the success of peaceful, organized protests across the South. They were following the nonviolent protest techniques used by Mahatma Gandhi in the 1930s during the struggle to free India from Britain's colonial rule.

On July 19, 1958, 19-year-old Carol Parks sat down on a lunch counter stool and ordered a soda at Dockhum Drugstore in Wichita, Kansas. Black customers were only allowed to order food for takeout. "You'd come in and go to the end of this counter and when you were served anything, it was in disposable containers," Parks later explained. "We never knew what it was to just sit there and have a glass and dishes." Other protesters walked in, occupying the restaurant's seats. The waitress refused to serve them. As NAACP youth leaders, Parks and her 20-year-old cousin Ron Walters had organized high school and college students to take shifts on lunch counter stools for weeks. Almost a month after the sit-in began, the owner "looked directly to his manager and he said, 'Serve them—I'm losing too much money,'" Parks remembered.

Two months before the Greensboro Four headed downtown, Martin Luther King Jr. announced that "a full-scale assault will be made upon discrimination and segregation in all forms. . . . We must employ new methods of struggle, involving the masses of our people." These masses of people included students

"As kids, we always wanted to know what water from a white water fountain tasted like . . ."

As a young NAACP youth leader, Ron Walters and his cousin organized lunch counter sit-ins. Decades later, he was honored for his work.

who grew up with segregation. The Greensboro Four knew the impact segregation had on their generation. Blair remembered that "As kids, we always wanted to know what water from a white water fountain tasted like—we thought it would taste like lemonade." By adulthood, curiosity had turned to anger. McCain described feeling "more angry than my parents and grandparents and all the other generations combined. I didn't hate anybody, but I just thought the system had betrayed me."

ChapterThree
BEHIND THE SCENES

It was no coincidence that a news photographer was waiting for the Greensboro Four on the sidewalk outside Woolworth's on the protest's first day. For years, Ralph Johns, the white owner of a clothing shop, had felt uncomfortable sitting at segregated restaurants and watching "many of my black friends walk by the window where I sat eating, and yet they could not enjoy the same privilege as a [white] American." He knew McNeil and other A&T students who shopped at his store. They often discussed what to do about segregation in Greensboro. The protesters visited his shop on the way to the Woolworth's lunch counter. Someone called the newspaper to make sure journalists did not miss the protest about to take place. Many think Johns made the call.

Indeed, Johns marveled at how images and news from Greensboro vaulted the protest into the public eye: "The local press sent out news, and national press and television gave it the push to grow as fast as it did. I did not envision this until three days later—realized this was big, a historical revolution that would make the world sit up and take notice."

Anger drove the four men to take such bold action. But they also had to master their fear. "I was the last one to sit down because I was the most afraid,"

"If someone had come up behind me and said 'Boo,' I would have fallen out of the chair."

Richmond said later. "If someone had come up behind me and said, 'Boo,' I would have fallen out of the chair." Blair explained that they were raised to be careful around white people and not "do anything to incite them to want to harm you." And many black people, particularly of the older generation, did not support them. A black kitchen employee who confronted the protesters on the first day warned, "It's people like you who make our race look bad."

But many teenage sit-in protesters had a different attitude than their parents. And their anger was stronger than their fear. When the Greensboro Four were about 14 years old, they saw unforgettable newspaper and television images: the brutalized face of a boy their same age and race. White men in Mississippi had beaten and then shot and killed Emmett Till. Some say it was because he insulted a white woman. "I remember seeing the picture of him when they pulled him out of the river," remembered Blair. "I never will forget that. It was chilling, bone-chilling." Mamie Till asked photographers to take photographs of her son in his coffin, despite his gruesome state. "Let the world see what I've seen," she said. Blair remembered thinking, "If we spoke out of turn, we too could die like Emmett Till." One of Till's killers later vowed to continue doing everything possible to make sure black Americans "are gonna stay in their place." Instead, the racist murder helped

create a new generation of determined civil-rights activists, both black and white.

Mamie Till had used photographers to tell a story many whites wanted to ignore. King also believed in the necessity of cameras, newspapers, and television in the civil rights struggle. In 1961 he wrote: "The world seldom believes the horror stories of history until they are documented via the mass media." Roberts said he took photographs because people needed to see "real-time, revealing pictures of the struggle ongoing among the races in the South."

Photographs also captured hopeful moments in the civil rights struggle. Greensboro's Gillespie Park Elementary School was one of the first segregated schools in the south to voluntarily accept black students. Moebes was there to photograph five black children on their first day of school there in 1957.

Roberts moved from his hometown of Mount Vernon, New York, to North Carolina in the mid-1950s, attracted by its reputation as a forward-looking southern state. But it didn't seem progressive to the Greensboro Four. They were not sure what would happen when they headed to the Woolworth's store on February 1. McNeil imagined spectators would be confused by their sit-in. "What they saw was a group of four teenagers and, 'How seriously do you want to take them?' was their approach," he explained years later. "They did not appreciate the depth of our seriousness and our anger and our wills to take this thing on."

Photographers could not capture the emotions behind the protesters' carefully composed expressions. As soon as Blair sat on the forbidden stools, he felt immediate relief, "like a great weight had been taken off my shoulder." McCain remembered "the most wonderful feeling . . . of liberation, restored manhood. . . . I truly felt almost invincible. . . ." As if this feeling were contagious, students from other colleges—male and female, black and white—joined protests spreading across Greensboro.

WOMEN OF THE GREENSBORO PROTEST

Women participated in the protests in large numbers. It was many years before they got as much attention as the male protesters did.

Photographs and news stories broke the story that four male students from A&T University began the Woolworth's protest. Women protesters from Bennett College also took stools in the following days. In the decades since, these women have told the story of how the roots of the protest could also be found at Bennett. Bennett was an all-black women's college, situated less than a mile from A&T University. Author and former Bennett student Linda Brown remembered that A&T students joined NAACP meetings at the Bennett campus, where plans for sit-ins were discussed for a year. The February 1 protest "was spontaneous in the sense that they decided to take the bull by the horns," Brown said, "but it was not that suddenly they woke up that day and it was a new idea."

Colleges and universities often disapproved of student protests and even punished the students by expelling them from school. But Bennett College President Willa Beatrice Player, the first black woman in the U.S. to head a four-year college, encouraged her students to be activists. She invited Martin Luther King Jr. to speak on campus in 1958 when no other group in Greensboro would. She set rules to help the nonviolent protests be effective. Her students had to make a store purchase before sitting down at a lunch counter and they had to complete nonviolence training. But Player strongly defended their right to protest once they had had that training.

Lunch counter manager Harris watched the protesters and scowled. He had started working for Woolworth's in college, and now managed one of the busiest Woolworth's lunch counters in the South. He vented his frustrations in his private journal, calling the protesters selfish for disrupting business, especially since he treated black employees well. What's more, since other downtown restaurants were segregated, Harris was frustrated that his store was targeted. "That was the practice," Harris wrote. "Why should Woolworth's be any different?"

Blair later described his appreciation of how Woolworth's handled the protest. While Kress, a similar type of store, had protesters arrested for trespassing, Woolworth's did not. Woolworth's Vice President Edward Harrigan explained that the company believed the protesters should be left alone since they were store customers and were behaving peacefully.

Harris glared at the protesters but did not threaten them. Even during the first days of the sit-in, Harris understood that his store would never be the same. "I knew that hundreds would be involved . . ." Harris wrote. "I knew then the eventual result: Woolworth's would serve [black customers], but it would have to be when the fury subsided." Blair once said, "I wish I could meet his grandchildren, to tell them just how much of a gentleman he was to us."

Protesters in New York City marched in support of those who protested segregated lunch counters in the South.

Meanwhile, state government officials criticized the protesters sharply and openly. "Such trouble-makers are irresponsible, and their actions can only result in irreparable harm being done to racial relations here in North Carolina," announced state Attorney General Malcolm Seawell. The Greensboro Four accepted the risks of a peaceful protest, as had Parks, King, and other activists before them. "We fully talked about the prospects of going to jail," McCain remembered. "In fact, we didn't think we'd come back to campus." But the Greensboro police became unlikely allies. Police chief Paul Calhoun stated, "As far as we were

Sometimes stores simply closed their lunch counters entirely rather than serve black people.

concerned, the people had a right to be in the store." When white opponents carrying signs with racial slurs and waving Confederate flags became disruptive—even throwing burning newspapers under protesters' stools—officers led them from the store.

Most white North Carolina residents did not witness lunch counter sit-ins, but their letters to government officials revealed how strongly—and how divided—they were about segregation. One letter reads, "Let's all sit together as human beings should." But others express indignation. "I am writing to urge you to do something about these disgusting "sit-down strikes," reads one letter. "Something terrible is going to happen if these Negroes are not kept out of the stores demanding service. . . ."

Newspapers rushed to keep up with the sit-in movement that grew day by day. Sit-ins spread across cities in North Carolina and neighboring Virginia, north up to Maryland, south to Florida, and west to Texas. The sit-ins soon became a national story. So when *Life* editor Ray Mackland heard that Charlotte students were protesting at Woolworth's on February 9, he made sure a photographer was on the scene.

As Roberts rushed into Charlotte's Woolworth's store, the last waitress was leaving, quietly turning over the lunch counter to the protesters. The students had informed the police chief about the protest and promised it would be peaceful. The protest leader, Charles Jones, remembered instructing protesters: "We will be dignified, we will not hit back, we will not talk a challenge, we will sit quietly with dignity, and we will continue to do that until we open up the lunch counter."

And they did. They juggled college classes with two-hour shifts at downtown lunch counters throughout the spring and into the summer. And each time black protesters occupied restaurant seats

"Something terrible is going to happen if these Negroes are not kept out of the stores demanding service . . ."

The movement to boycott Woolworth's spread throughout the nation.

reserved for white customers, businesses lost money.

Black people in Charlotte knew their power and launched a boycott of all downtown businesses. Business owners feared losing white customers if they integrated, but now they were losing black customers—in Greensboro, that meant one-quarter of the population. Small local businesses could not afford such losses. Charlotte business owners finally gave in.

To mark the change, a new kind of staged event took place in Greensboro, on Woolworth's lunch counter stools, on July 25, 1960. This time black student leaders and white business owners planned it together. To avoid triggering conflict in the city, newspapers agreed to wait until after it was over to report on it.

In Woolworth's, four black employees changed out of their kitchen uniforms into their own clothes. One of them, Geneva Tisdale, had found the boldness of the sit-ins alarming at first. For nearly a decade, she had prepared food for white customers and hadn't questioned the injustice of the segregated counter. She explained, "That's the way things were at that time. And I was used to that." But when the protest "got started, then I got to thinking about it. . . . We fixed all the food that went down, and then we couldn't sit and be served ourselves." Now she sat with her coworkers to receive service as customers. Tisdale nervously ate an egg sandwich. She heard whispering behind her as others saw the unusual sight of black customers eating at the lunch counter. "Everybody had to get used to these new roles," she recalled. Tisdale was proud of her role. Customers in the store that day "never knew that it was Woolworth's girls that [were] the first to sit at the counter to be served after they opened it up."

ChapterFour
A PEACEFUL WAR

Soon after the Greensboro Four began their protest in early February 1960, John Lewis remembered a telephone ringing in Nashville, Tennessee. Lewis was a Fisk University student at the time. He recalled a North Carolina student on the line asking, "What can you do to support the students in Greensboro?" Black students at Nashville universities were more than ready to help. "No longer did we have to explain nonviolence to people," said CORE leader and civil rights activist James Farmer. "Thanks to Martin Luther King, it was a household word." Since 1958 James Lawson, a theology student at Nashville's Vanderbilt University, had held workshops to prepare protesters for sit-ins. Through role-playing, participants practiced not giving in to hatred or anger even while facing abuse and humiliation. Their power as peaceful protesters lay in staying calm and keeping their minds focused on the goal.

Rehearsal time ended on February 13, 1960. The first day of the Nashville protests was dramatic compared to the quiet start of the Greensboro protests. Not four, but 124, protesters walked into downtown Nashville's Woolworth's and two other stores, made purchases, and sat calmly at the whites-only counters. The manager closed the store,

but protesters returned the next day, quietly taking
shifts. "When you see something that is not right, not
fair, not just," said Lewis, then 19, "you have a moral
obligation, a mission, and a mandate, to stand up,
to speak up and speak out, and get in the way, get
in trouble, good trouble, necessary trouble." Trouble
arrived two weeks later. A group of whites pulled
protesters off stools and beat them. When police
arrived, they arrested more than 80 protesters. Not
one of the white attackers was arrested. Jail did not
intimidate 21-year-old sit-in leader Diane Nash: "I

"I want a good America and I want that just a little bit more than a college degree."

want a good America and I want that just a little bit more than a college degree." The risk of jail did not stop more students from joining the Nashville sit-ins.

In April a bomb destroyed the Nashville home of Z. Alexander Looby, a black lawyer defending the protesters. Outraged sit-in leaders marched with thousands to City Hall, where Nash confronted the mayor outside. He admitted that segregation of lunch counters should end. Nashville protesters saw the results of their efforts even before Greensboro did. By May 10, Nashville lunch counters began serving black customers. But sit-ins were part of a movement bringing changes across the South. Lewis later emphasized that sit-ins required that the "total community, every segment of the black community, get involved." By the end of April 1960, more than 50,000 students had sat on lunch counter stools in protests across the South. Even in northern cities such as Boston and New York, supporters formed picket lines at chain stores like Woolworth's that permitted segregation in their southern stores.

Sit-ins grew into an unstoppable movement. King assumed that young student leaders would join SCLC, his civil rights organization. But these young people were restless for change. "We didn't trust anybody over 18," said Greensboro Four member Ezell Blair, who later changed his name to Jibreel Khazan when he became a member of the New England Islamic

Center. College campuses became the center of
the civil rights movement. Civil rights leader Ella
Baker invited student leaders to Shaw University in
Raleigh, North Carolina, in April 1960. More than 200
students representing 12 southern states—including
Charlotte's Charles Jones and Nashville's John Lewis
and Diane Nash—formed the Student Nonviolent
Coordinating Committee (SNCC).

King respected the young SNCC activists'
desire for independence. But he and other older,
experienced leaders would continue to lend support.
In Greensboro the NAACP promised to offer lawyers

The members
of SNCC worked
tirelessly to
plan civil rights
marches and
demonstrations.

to defend protesters in court, if necessary. The protesters themselves reached out to CORE leaders for guidance on how to organize the protest as it grew into a national movement. In Atlanta, Georgia, King would even take a stool alongside protesters, despite a threat by Georgia government officials to take him to court if he caused any disorder.

News from Greensboro spurred Georgia government officials to pass a law making it illegal for anyone to remain after store managers asked them to leave. But 23-year-old Lonnie King, a student at Morehouse College in Atlanta, had already told his friends, "Let's follow Greensboro." He and classmate Julian Bond began planning a sit-in campaign at local lunch counters. But first they announced their goals. On March 9 a local paper printed a detailed statement signed by student leaders at Atlanta's six all-black colleges and universities: "We . . . have joined our hearts, minds, and bodies in the cause of gaining those rights which are inherently ours as members of the human race and as citizens of these United States. . . . We do not intend to wait placidly for those rights which are already legally and morally ours to be meted out to us one at a time." Days later *The New York Times* printed a section of the statement and it went national.

On March 15, 1960, 200 students targeted 10 different Atlanta locations with sit-ins of lunch counters, government buildings, and bus and train stations. No violence erupted during the massive protest. The NAACP swept in to help with the courtroom battles of the 77 protesters who were arrested. Yet there were frightening reminders of how easily a peaceful protest could turn brutal. In May police with dogs blocked several thousand protesters marching toward the state capitol building.

Atlanta protesters had two powerful weapons. The first was a boycott launched in June that may have cost Atlanta stores millions of dollars. The second was the participation of Atlanta resident Martin Luther King Jr. in the sit-ins that had been going on since March 1960. When King and about 280 students were arrested on October 19, it had an impact well beyond Atlanta. The nation was two weeks from the 1960 presidential election. Democratic candidate John F. Kennedy called King's wife to show his concern, while his brother Robert, a lawyer, intervened to release the jailed civil rights hero. More than 70 percent of black people voted for Kennedy, helping him achieve victory in a close race with Republican candidate Richard Nixon.

Atlanta's white business owners finally agreed in March 1961 to begin desegregating. By 1962 protests had taken place in more than 120 cities in 13 states. The protests also spread beyond lunch counters. In the two years since the Greensboro Four first sat

Atlanta's white business owners finally agreed in March 1961 to begin desegregating.

Martin Luther King Jr. (right) was arrested for taking part in an Atlanta sit-in.

down in protest, hundreds of businesses desegregated after protesters headed to whites-only pools, parks, churches, theaters, and libraries to launch wade-ins, walk-ins, kneel-ins, and read-ins. Sit-ins helped turn

YOUNG PROTESTERS TAKE CHARGE

Ella Baker encouraged students to organize without waiting for older people to tell them how to do so.

Longtime activist Ella Baker grew up hearing powerful stories from her grandmother, who had once been enslaved. During the 1940s, she traveled the South with the NAACP, organizing campaigns for equal wages for black people, school integration, and other civil rights issues. Rosa Parks had participated in one of her workshops. In 1958 Baker moved to Atlanta to help launch the Southern Christian Leadership Conference (SCLC), but she soon clashed with the group's leader, Martin Luther King Jr. She felt the organization focused too little on its goals and too much on King himself.

When sit-in protests began spreading across the South, Baker saw a new opportunity. She believed that "the young people were the hope of any movement." In April 1960, the 56-year-old gathered student leaders at the college where she had graduated three decades earlier, Shaw University in Raleigh, North Carolina. During the two-day meeting, Baker encouraged them to organize and to depend on each other rather than on SCLC. They formed the Student Nonviolent Coordinating Committee (SNCC). She later explained, "The major job was getting people to understand that they had something within their power that they could use . . . and how group action could counter violence."

James Lawson, leader of Nashville's nonviolent workshops, wrote a statement showing that the new group would still follow the same path of nonviolence as older groups like CORE and SCLC: "Through nonviolence, courage displaces fear; love transforms hate. Acceptance dissipates prejudice; hopes ends despair. . . . By appealing to conscience and standing on the moral nature of human existence, nonviolence nurtures the atmosphere in which reconciliation and justice become actual possibilities."

young talented protesters into leaders. (John Lewis later become—and remains—a congressman.)

In early 1963 King directed protestors' focus to Alabama's capital, Birmingham, which he called the most segregated city in the nation. Young people once again stepped into risky positions in the campaign. The sit-ins, boycotts, and marches demanded a steady supply of volunteers. SCLC and local leaders recruited college and high school students. "Don't worry about your children; they're going to be all right," King assured parents. "Don't hold them back if they want to go to jail, for they are doing a job for not only themselves, but for all of America and for all mankind." At least 900 students between the ages of 6 and 16 skipped school on May 2 to march downtown. Police interrupted them and jailed hundreds. Hundreds more gathered to march the next day. This time Police Commissioner Bull Connor ordered the young activists stopped with force.

Photographers and television crews made sure the nation and the world knew what happened to the child activists in Birmingham. Roberts explained that "the more people who saw these photographs the better. Little-by-little these readers considered that maybe, just maybe, the encouragement of discrimination was not the way the South wanted to be portrayed to the rest of the nation and world." Firefighters blasted the activists with high-pressure hoses and police attacked with dogs and clubs.

President Kennedy told a stunned nation in 1963 that "the events in Birmingham and elsewhere have so increased the cries for equality that no city or state or legislative body can prudently choose to ignore them." The next day Medgar Evers, an NAACP member organizing boycotts and demonstrations in Mississippi—in addition to investigating the murder of Emmett Till—was murdered by a white opponent of civil rights. Kennedy followed the promise he made in his address. He urged Congress to pass a law that finally ensured that all Americans could freely use all public places.

Violence against protesters grabbed international attention—as did 250,000 black and white citizens

A quarter-million people marched on Washington, D.C., in 1963.

marching peacefully in Washington, D.C., on August 28, 1963. There, King delivered his "I Have a Dream" speech. SNCC chairman Lewis was the youngest speaker. "Those who have said be patient and wait—we must say that we cannot be patient," said the 23-year-old. "We do not want our freedom gradually. But we want to be free now." Hope filled the gathering. Kennedy submitted a civil rights bill to Congress.

Southern state governments were against the civil rights bill. Kennedy's assassination on November 22, 1963, left the job of supporting the bill to new President Lyndon B. Johnson. The longtime politician from the south helped persuade southern congressmen to support the bill. On July 2, in a ceremony broadcast on national TV networks, President Johnson signed the Civil Rights Act into law. Civil rights leaders, including Parks and King, looked on. Protesters who decades earlier had formed picket lines outside northern stores that did not hire black people finally had the federal government on their side. Federal law now made it illegal to deny anyone a job because of his or her race. Protesters who had sat in segregated restaurants, libraries, and other segregated public places now had the federal government on their side too. Federal law also made segregation illegal in all public spaces.

Photographers such as Roberts continued to document the journey toward equality in all its forms. Inside a newly integrated school in 1966, Roberts photographed black and white children playing together "as if segregation had never existed." Yet Roberts and other photojournalists also rushed with their cameras to protests to capture the difficulty of the civil rights struggle—which many believe is not only dangerous to forget but still ongoing.

On February 1, 1990, 30 years after the sit-ins, a crowd of journalists and spectators packed the Woolworth's lunch counter in Greensboro. The Greensboro Four sat together at the counter on the 30th anniversary of their protest. To honor the men, Woolworth's executive Aubrey Lewis, who is

"You had the courage to open the door for an entire movement."

The Greensboro Four at the 30th anniversary of their protest. From left, McNeil, Khazan (formerly Blair Jr.), McCain, and Richmond.

black, traveled from New York to help serve them breakfast with the help of Geneva Tisdale. "You had the courage to open the door for an entire movement. Thirty years ago, you could not be served here. I could not be served here," said Lewis. "But because of what you did, I now stand here as vice president of Woolworth's."

Timeline

1868

The 14th amendment to the U.S. Constitution in 1868 grants citizenship and equal rights to all, including people newly freed from slavery

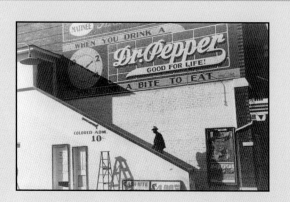

1896

The U.S. Supreme Court rules in *Plessy v. Ferguson* that segregation is constitutional as long as black and white citizens have access to facilities that are of equal quality

1942

CORE is founded in Chicago by James Farmer and a group of black and white activists

1954

The *Brown v. Board of Education* Supreme Court decision reverses *Plessy v. Ferguson* by ruling that segregation in public schools is unconstitutional

1909

The NAACP is founded by white and black activists in response to violence against black people and to promote political, economic, educational, and social equality

1939

Samuel Tucker organizes sit-in protest at a whites-only library in Alexandria, Virginia. A separate library for black patrons is created, but that solution does not address the segregation problem in that southern city

1955

Rosa Parks is arrested for her bus protest in Montgomery, Alabama. On the day her trial begins, Martin Luther King Jr. mobilizes the black community to launch a bus boycott that lasts more than a year

Timeline

1958

Sit-in campaigns launched in Wichita, Kansas, and then Oklahoma City, Oklahoma, target store chains

1960

On February 1, Ezell Blair Jr., Joseph McNeil, David Richmond, and Franklin McCain begin a sit-in at a Woolworth's lunch counter in Greensboro, North Carolina

1964

Congress passes the Civil Rights Act, which allows the government to enforce desegregation of public spaces

1960

In April SNCC is founded at Shaw University in Raleigh, North Carolina

1963

On August 28 King leads a peaceful March on Washington in support of the Civil Rights bill with SNCC chairman. John Lewis as the youngest speaker.

On November 22, President John F. Kennedy is assassinated in Dallas, Texas

1968

On April 4 Martin Luther King Jr. is assassinated in Memphis, Tennessee

1990

A ceremony is held at Woolworth's to celebrate the 30th anniversary of the Greensboro Four protest

Glossary

activist—a person who works for political or social change

amendment—a formal change made to a law or legal document, such as the U.S. Constitution

boycott—to refuse to buy or use a product or service to protest something believed to be wrong or unfair

chain—when related to businesses, a series of stores owned by one business and offering the same items and services

civil rights—legal rights guaranteed to every citizen of a country relating to such things as voting and receiving equal treatment

Confederate—relating to the Southern states that fought against the Northern states in the Civil War

desegregate—to end by law the isolation of members of a particular race or ethnicity

discrimination—the unfair treatment of a person or group because of race, religion, gender, sexual preference, or age

moral—a belief about what is right and wrong behavior

progressive—in favor of improvement, progress, and reform, especially in political or social matters

recruit—to ask someone to join a company, organization, or social or political movement

segregation—the practice of separating people of different races, classes, ethnicities, or genders

unconstitutional—a law that goes against something set forth in the U.S. Constitution

Additional Resources

Further Reading

Clayton, Ed. *Martin Luther King: The Peaceful Warrior*. Candlewick Press, 2017.

Lusted, Marcia Amidon. *Civic Unrest: Investigate the Struggle for Social Change*. Inquire and Investigate. Nomad Press, 2015.

Osborne, Linda Barrett. *Miles to Go for Freedom: Segregation and Civil Rights in the Jim Crow Years*. Abrams Books for Young Readers, 2016.

Williams, Lea E. *We Who Believe in Freedom: The Life and Times of Ella Baker*. True Tales for Young Readers. Raleigh: North Carolina Office of Archives and History, 2017.

Internet Sites

Use FactHound to find Internet sites related to this book.
Visit *www.facthound.com*
Just type in 9780756558338 and go.

Critical Thinking Questions

Young activists were impatient with what Atlanta protesters called the "snail-like speed" of progress in the courtrooms. In what ways was nonviolent protest a better strategy? In what ways was it not?

The sit-in movement was the training ground for history-making civil rights leaders. What qualities did they demonstrate while organizing sit-ins that made them effective? Consider John Lewis, Samuel Tucker, Diane Nash, James Farmer, or Mary Church Terrell, among others.

The Civil Rights Act of 1964 was a landmark in civil rights but racial relations are still tense in the United States. Why do you think this might be, and what do you think might help ease the tension? Would protest, voting, or legislation be most effective? Use evidence from the text to support your answer.

Source Notes

p. 4, "We're going to do something…" Dr. Steven Channing and Rebecca Cerese. *February One: The Story of the Greensboro Four*, 2003. [video]

p. 4, Do you guys realize?" Ibid.

p. 6, "Are you chicken?" Ibid.

p. 9, "Why don't you boys?" Jim Schlosser. "Four Men Summon Courage to Alter Course of History." *Greensboro News & Record*, January 27, 1985, http://www.greensboro.com/sit-ins/headlines/four-men-summon-courage-to-alter-course-of-history/article_4c03b8b0-e321-11e6-959c-d337089cdae0.html

p. 10, "seeking luncheon counter service…" "Greensboro, NC, Students sit-in for U.S. Civil Rights, 1960." Global Noviolent Action Database, https://nvdatabase.swarthmore.edu/content/greensboro-nc-students-sit-us-civil-rights-1960

p. 11, "It wasn't as though…" *February One: The Story of the Greensboro Four.*

p. 13, "where the rules of life were very clear…" Debbie Howard. "Interview with J. Charlie Jones." UNC Charlotte, http://nsv.uncc.edu/interview/bbjo0025

p. 14, "waiting peacefully to see what would happen…" "Women's Sit-In Charlotte Woolworth's." Bruce Roberts Photography, http://bruceroberts photography.com/Page27.html

p. 14, "one of the quietest things I've ever photographed…" Jeff Hampton. "N.C. Photojournalist's Work to be Exhibited," *The Virginian Pilot*, https://pilotonline.com/news/n-c-photojournalist-s-work-to-be-exhibited/article_636b666f-731e-5f1c-af19-6e0a931534bc.html

p. 15, "opened up a whole new beautiful world…" Richard Maschal. "Book Reveals Photographer's Images of North Carolina's Tumultuous 1950s and '60s." *News & Observer*, http://www.newsobserver.com/entertainment/books/article10865651.html

p. 15, "Eventually many other photographers…" Richard Maschal, "Book Reveals Photographer's Images of North Carolina's Tumultuous 1950s and '60s.

p. 16, "You will treat me …"*February One: The Story of the Greensboro Four.*

pp. 18-19 , "Our constitution is color-blind…" Charles Thompson. "*Plessy v. Ferguson: Harlan's Great Dissent.*" Louis D. Brandeis School of Law Library, https://louisville.edu/law/library/special-collections/the-john-marshall-harlan-collection/harlans-great-dissent

p. 23, "without fear, without compromise…" Helene Slessarev-Jamir. *Prophetic Activism: Progressive Religious Justice Movements in Contemporary America*. Religion and Social Transformation. New York: NYU Press, 2011.

p. 27, "While the Montgomery boycott…" Martin Luther King, Jr. "My Trip to the Land of Gandhi." *King Encyclopedia*, December 1, 1959, http://kingencyclopedia.stanford.edu/encyclopedia/documentsentry/sclc_press_release_dr_king_leaves_montgomery_for_atlanta/

p. 28, "a full scale assault …" "Dr. King Leaves Montgomery for Atlanta." *King Encyclopedia.*

p. 29, "As kids, we always wanted to know…" Jim Schlosser. "Four Men Summon Courage to Alter Course of History," *Greensboro News & Record*, January 27, 1985, http://www.greensboro.com/sit-ins/headlines/four-men-summon-courage-to-alter-course-of-history/article_4c03b8b0-e321-11e6-959c-d337089cdae0.html

p. 29, "more angry than my…" *February One: The Story of the Greensboro Four*, 2003.

p. 30, "many of my black friends…" Eugene Pfaff. "Oral History Interview with Ralph Johns." UNCG Digital Collections, January 17, 1979, http://libcdm1.uncg.edu/cdm/ref/collection/CivilRights/id/843

p. 30, "The local press sent out news…" "Oral History Interview with Jo Spivey."

pp. 30-31, "I was the last one to sit down…"Eugene Pfaff. "Oral History Interview with Ralph Johns."

p. 31, "do anything to incite them to want to harm you…" "Four Men Summon Courage to Alter Course of History."

p. 31, "It's people like you who make our race look bad…" Ibid.

p. 31, "I remember seeing the picture of him…"*February One: The Story of the Greensboro Four.*

p. 31, "Let the world see what I've seen…" Maurice Berger. "The Lasting Power of Emmett Till's Image." *The New York Times*, April 5, 2017, https://lens.blogs.nytimes.com/2017/04/05/controversy-contexts-using-emmett-tills-image/?mcubz=1&_r=0

p. 31, "are gonna stay in their place…" Jennifer Latson. "How Emmett Till's Murder Changed the World." *TIME*, August 28, 2015, http://time.com/4008545/emmett-till-history/

p. 31, "if we spoke out of turn…" *February One: The Story of the Greensboro Four.*

p. 32, "real-time, revealing pictures of the struggle…"Bruce Roberts. November 27, 2017. Email Interview.

p. 33, "What they saw was a group of four teenagers…." Nancy McLaughlin. "Clarence 'Curly' Harris had 'fifth seat' at Greensboro sit-ins." *Greensboro News & Record*, January 31, 2014, http://www.greensboro.com/news/local_news/clarence-curly-harris-had-fifth-seat-at-greensboro-sit-ins/article_3fad3bb6-8af7-11e3-a0a9-0017a43b2370.html

p. 33, "like a great weight…"*February One: The Story of the Greensboro Four.*

p. 33, "the most wonderful feeling…" Michele Norris, "The Woolworth's Sit-In That Launched a Movement." NPR, February 1, 2008, https://www.npr.org/templates/story/story.php?storyId=18615556

p. 34, "was spontaneous…" "Linda Beatrice Brown: Greensboro Sit-Ins." C-SPAN. Online Video, June 22, 2016.

p. 35, "That was the practice…" "Clarence 'Curly' Harris had 'fifth seat' at Greensboro sit-ins."

p. 35, "I wish I could meet his grandchildren…" Ibid.

p. 35, "I knew then the eventual result…" *February One The Story of the Greensboro Four.*

p. 36, "Such trouble-makers …" "Documents Highlight Response to Sit-Ins." NC Department of Natural and Cultural Resources, https://www.ncdcr.gov/blog/2016/02/01/documents-highlight-response-to-sit-ins

p. 36, "We fully talked about the prospects of going to jail…" "Four Men Summon Courage to Alter Course of History"

p. 38, "Let's all sit together…" Katrina Martin. "Let's All Sit Together: Greensboro Citizens Respond to the 1960 Sit-Ins in the Edward R. Zane Papers." Duke University Libraries, February 11, 2016. https://blogs.library.duke.edu/rubenstein/2016/02/11/greensboro-sit-ins/

p. 38, "I am writing to urge you…" "Letter: Kathleen Lindsay to Governor Luther H. Hodges, March 1, 1960." UNCG Digital Collections, March 1, 1960. http://digital.ncdcr.gov/cdm/compoundobject/collection/p16062coll17/id/352/rec/8

p. 38, "We will be dignified…"Debbie Howard. "Interview with J. Charles Jones. UNC Charlotte, May 18, 2005, http://nsv.uncc.edu/interview/bbjo0025

p. 40, "that's the way things were…" "Oral History Interview with Geneva Tisdale."

p. 40, "Everybody had to get used to…"Nancy McLaughlin. "Blacks First Served in Restaurants 50 Years Ago Today." *Greensboro News & Record*, July 24, 2010, http://www.greensboro.com/news/blacks-first-served-in-restaurants-years-ago-today/article_e600ce7b-5748-5b08-89d2-b2fee6957552.html

p. 40, "never knew…" "Oral History Interview with Geneva Tisdale, https://www.c-span.org/video/?c4606141/linda-beatrice-brown-greensboro-sit-ins

p. 41, "What can you do?" "Interview with John Lewis, November 20, 1973." Documenting the American South, November 20, 1973. http://docsouth.unc.edu/sohp/A-0073/A-0073.html

p. 41, "No longer did we have to explain…" Ron Grossman. "The Birth of the Sit-In." *Chicago Tribune*, February 23, 2014.

p. 41, "Thanks to Martin Luther King…" Ibid.

p. 41, "Through role-playing…" "Jim Lawson Conducts Nonviolence Workshops in Nashville." SNCC Digital, https://snccdigital.org/events/jim-lawson-conducts-nonviolent-workshops-in-nashville/

p. 42, "When you see something that is not right…" Tony Gonzalez. "In Nashville, Rep. John Lewis Gets Surprise from His Civil Rights Past." NPR, November 21, 2016, https://www.npr.org/2016/11/21/502918030/in-nashville-rep-john-lewis-gets-surprise-from-his-civil-rights-past

p. 43, "I want a good America…" "Documenting the American South.

p. 43, "We didn't trust anybody over 18…" *February One: The Story of the Greensboro Four.*

p. 45, "Let's follow Greensboro…" "Lonnie C. King: The Second Battle for Atlanta". 60s Survivors, March 14, 2018 http://sixtiessurvivors.org/king.html

Source Notes

p. 48, "the young people were the hope of the movement..." "EllaBaker," SNCC Digital, https://snccdigital. org/people/ella-baker/

p. 48, "The major job was getting people to understand..." "Student Nonviolent Coordinating Committee (SNCC)."

p. 48, "Through nonviolence courage displaces fear...""Student Nonviolent Coordinating Committee Statement of Purpose." National Humanities Center. 14 Mar 2018. http://nationalhumanitiescenter. org/pds/maai3/protest/text2/snccstatementofpurpose.pdf

p. 49, "Don't worry about your children..." "Birmingham Campaign (1963)." *King Encyclopedia.*

p. 49, "the more people who saw these photographs the better..." Bruce Roberts. Email interview

p. 50, "the events in Birmingham and elsewhere have so increased the crites for equality..." "Report to the American People on Civil Rights," June 11, 1963, John F. Kennedy Presidential Library and Museum." https://www.jfklibrary.org/Asset-Viewer/LH8F_0Mzv0e6Ro1yEm74Ng.aspx

p. 51, "Those who have said be patient..." Allison Keyes, "50 Years After March on Washington, John Lewis Still Fights," August 27, 2013, https://www.npr.org/2013/08/28/216259218/50-years-after-march-on-washington-john-lewis-still-fighting

p. 53, "as if segregation had never existed..." Bruce Roberts. *Just Yesterday in North Carolina: People and Places.* Sarsasota, Fla: Pineapple Press, 2014.

p. 53, "You had the courage..." "Four Men Summon Courage to Alter Course of History."

p. 53, "But because of what you did..." Terry Donahue. "Woolworth's Serves Breakfast to Civil Rights Instigators." UPI, February 1, 1990, https://www.upi.com/Archives/1990/02/01/Woolworth'ss-serves-breakfast-to-civil-rights-instigators/2770633848400/

All Internet sites accessed March 14, 2018

Select Bibliography

Adler, Margot, "Before Rosa Parks, There was Claudette Colvin." NPR. March 15, 2009, https://www.npr.org/2009/03/15/101719889/before-rosa-parks-there-was-claudette-colvin Accessed March 14, 2018

Alston, Melvin, "Greensboro Sit-Ins, Jason Ins at Woolworth's, February-July 1960." UNCG Digital Collections, July 1960, http://libcdm1.uncg.edu/cdm/essay1960/collection/CivilRights Accessed March 14, 2018

Channing, Steven, and Rebecca Ceres. *February One: The Story of the Greensboro Four*, 2003. [video]

Edwards, Owen, "Courage at the Greensboro Lunch Counter." *Smithsonian*, February 2010, https://www.smithsonianmag.com/arts-culture/courage-at-the-greensboro-lunch-counter-4507661/ Accessed March 14, 2018

Eschner, Kat, "Martin Luther King and Gandhi Weren't the Only Ones Inspired by Throeau's 'Civil Disobedience.'" *Smithsonian*, July 12, 2017, https://www.smithsonianmag.com/smart-news/martin-luther-king-and-gandhi-werent-only-ones-inspired-thoreaus-civil-disobedience-180963972/ Accessed March 14, 2018

Gallagher, Charles. *Race and Racism in the United States: An Encyclopedia of the American Mosaic*. Santa Barbara, Calif.: Greenwood, 2014.

Garber, Paul. "Former Leader Guided Police: Paul Calhoun, Who Died Saturday, Spent More Than 30 Years in the Department – Many of them as its Chief," *Greensboro News & Record*, January 19, 2002, http://www.greensboro.com/former-leader-guided-police-paul-calhoun-who-died-saturday-spent/

article_bc22b49a-6b7c-5b20-84a0-4298cd9d052c.html Accessed March 14, 2018

Howard, Debbie. "Interview with J. Charles Jones." UNC Charlotte J. Murrey Atkins Library, http://nsv.uncc.edu/interview/bbjo0025 Accessed March 14, 2018

McLaughlin, Nancy. "Clarence 'Curly' Harris had 'fifth seat' at Greensboro sit-ins." *Greensboro News & Record*, January 31, 2014. http://www.greensboro.com/news/local_news/clarence-curly-harris-had-fifth-seat-at-greensboro-sit-ins/article_3fad3bb6-8af7-11e3-a0a9-0017a43b2370.html Accessed March 14, 2018

Norris, Michele, "The Woolworth's Sit-In That Launched a Movement." NPR, February 1, 2008, https://www.npr.org/templates/story/story.php?storyId=18615556

Pfaff, Eugene. "Oral History Interview with Jack Moebes," UNCG Digital Collections, April 18, 1979. 871 Accessed March 14, 2018

Pfaff, Eugene. "Oral History Interview with Ralph Johns and Jack Moebes," UNCG Digital Collections, January 17, 1979, http://libcdm1.uncg.edu/cdm/ref/collection/CivilRights/id/843 Accessed March 14, 2018

Riley, Michael. "Greensboro, North Carolina The Legacy of Segregation." *TIME*, June 25, 1990, http://content.time.com/time/magazine/article/0,9171,970458,00.html Accessed March 14, 2018

Schlosser, Jim. "Oral History Interview with Geneva Tisdale." UNCG Digital Collections, January 1998, http://libcdm1.uncg.edu/cdm/ref/collection/CivilRights/id/911 Accessed March 14, 2018

Slessarev-Jamir, Helene. *Prophetic Activism: Progressive Religious Justice Movements in Contemporary America*. Religion and Social Transformation. New York: NYU Press, 2011.

Sullivan, Patricia. "Lawyer Samuel Tucker and his Historic 1939 Sit-In at Segregated Alexandria Library," *Washington Post*, August 7, 2014, https://www.washingtonpost.com/local/lawyer-samuel-tucker-and-his-historic-1939-sit-in-at-segregated-alexandria-library/2014/08/05/c9c1d38e-1be8-11e4-ae54-0cfe1f974f8a_story.html?utm_term=.19fda82d9e40 Accessed March 14, 2018

Wolcott, Victoria. *Race, Riots and Roller Coasters: The Struggle over Segregated Recreation in America*. Philadelphia, Pa.: University of Pennsylvania Press, 2014.

Index

About the Author

As a teacher, Danielle Smith-Llera taught children to think and write about literature before writing books for them herself. As the spouse of a diplomat, she has enjoyed the opportunity to live in Washington, D.C., and abroad. In writing this book, she was delighted to discover that she grew up near Ella Baker's hometown.